Effective Presentation Skills

A Practical Guide for Better Speaking

Third Edition

Steve Mandel

A Fifty-Minute™ Series Book

Effective Presentation Skills
A Practical Guide for Better Speaking

Third Edition

Steve Mandel

CREDITS:
Senior Editor: **Debbie Woodbury**
Copy Editor: **Charlotte Bosarge**
Production Manager: **Judy Petry**
Text Design: **Amy Shayne**
Layout: **Kay Green**
Cover: **Amy Shayne & 5th Street Design**
Artwork: **Ralph Mapson**

Printed in the United States of America by Von Hoffmann Graphics, Inc.

CrispLearning.com

04 05 06 07 12 11 10 9 8

This book is printed on recyclable paper with soy ink.

Library of Congress Catalog Card Number 99-69618
Mandel, Steve
Effective Presentation Skills, Third Edition
A Practical Guide for Better Speaking
ISBN 1-56052-526-6

Learning Objectives For:

Effective Presentation Skills

Third Edition

The objectives for *Effective Presentation Skills—Third Edition* are listed below. They have been developed to guide you, the reader, to the core issues covered in this book.

THE OBJECTIVES OF THIS BOOK ARE:

❑ 1) To explain how to build credibility and confidence as a speaker

❑ 2) To show how to use presentation technology to your advantage

❑ 3) To provide techniques for preparing and delivering a presentation well

ASSESSING YOUR PROGRESS

In addition to the learning objectives, Crisp Learning has developed an **assessment** that covers the fundamental information presented in this book. A 25-item, multiple-choice and true-false questionnaire allows the reader to evaluate his or her comprehension of the subject matter. To buy the assessment and answer key, go to www.CrispLearning.com and search on the book title, or call 1-800-442-7477.

Assessments should not be used in any employee selection process.

About the Author

Steve Mandel, President of Frontline Group/Mandel Communications, is a nationally known training consultant and lecturer specializing in presentation skills training. Since 1981 his company has trained executives, managers, and professionals nationwide in the skills necessary to effectively present their ideas.

After graduate studies in Speech Communications, Mr. Mandel was an instructor and administrator for the University of California. He developed training programs in the areas of business management, finance, computer science, engineering, and management skills training for the University Extension division.

Mr. Mandel is the author of two Crisp books, *Effective Presentation Skills* and *Technical Presentation Skills*, as well as numerous articles. He has also been a featured speaker for organizations on the topic of management communication skills in the professional environment.

For more information:

A two-day workshop based on the material in this book and the author's other Fifty-Minute book, *Technical Presentation Skills*, is available from Frontline Group/ Mandel Communications. Please contact us for more information at:

Frontline Group/Mandel Communications
610 Capitola Avenue
Capitola, CA 95010
1-800-262-6335
smandel@mandelcom.com

Dedication

This book is dedicated to those who helped make it happen and without whose support it would not exist: my wonderful wife Carol, my kids Joe, Paul and Alex, my colleagues at Frontline Group/Mandel Communications, and all the folks at Crisp Publications.

To the Reader

There is a myth that great speakers are born, "not made," that somehow certain individuals have the innate ability to stand in front of an audience with no anxiety, and give a moving, dynamic speech. Well, that just isn't so!

People we consider great speakers usually have spent years developing and practicing their skill. They had to start at the beginning and learn the basics of organization, preparation, delivery, and dealing with anxiety. Once the basics were in hand, they had to continue to build their abilities.

Professional athletes constantly practice the basics because they know that without such practice they will not survive. To an outsider, the thought of a professional golfer, for example, spending hour upon hour practicing the basics seems ridiculous. But to that professional, the mastery of those basic skills are the very foundation of success.

Learning to be a better speaker is similar to learning any activity. In the beginning it can be frustrating. After a few lessons in which you learn some theory and practice some of the basic skills, things usually improve. To really learn to do anything well takes constant practice and mastery of the basics.

Speaking is no different. Before becoming comfortable as a speaker, you need to learn some basic skills and then actively seek places to practice those skills. This may mean walking into your manager's office and volunteering to give more presentations, or joining a speaking club which allows you to speak in an organized setting. The more experience you gain, the more proficient and comfortable you will become.

Good luck!

Contents

Part 4: New Technology for Presentations

Part 5: Preparing Your Presentation

Part 6: Delivering Your Presentation with Energy and Composure

Preface

The study of how to give effective speeches dates back to ancient Greece. Around 350 B.C. Aristotle wrote his famous Rhetoric, now considered to be one of the finest formal books on the subject. Now 2,300 years later, we are still struggling with the same problems the Greeks encountered and that speakers have struggled with throughout the ages.

The advent of technology has both complicated and simplified the task of the speaker. For example, today it is possible to produce complex graphs on a computer, display them electronically with a projector, or present them via the Internet. But how much information should be put on that graph? And, most important, where does that graph fit into the organizational plan (if there is one) of the presentation?

Effective Presentation Skills attempts to answer the fundamental questions of how to prepare and deliver an effective speech. Proven techniques are presented that will give a reader the necessary skills to give more confident, enthusiastic and persuasive presentations. Topics covered are how to use body language effectively; how to organize thoughts and data for maximum impact; how to develop and use visuals and graphics, as well as (of course) how to deliver what you have prepared.

This book provides some theory but more often presents simple and practical suggestions on how to give more effective presentations.

Definitions

The terms "speech" and "presentation" are often used interchangeably. For our purposes it is useful to understand the difference.

A presentation is a type of speech. Typically, when we think of a speech we think of a dedication speech, a political speech, a speech of tribute, or some similar event that is more public in nature than a presentation would be.

Presentations are speeches that are usually given in a business, technical, professional, or scientific environment. The audience is likely to be more specialized than those attending a typical speech event.

Although the difference between speeches and presentations is slight, this book leans toward helping those who give presentations. But, because a presentation is a type of speech, there are ideas and skills in this book that will also be helpful to any speech-maker.

Assessing Your Skills

2

Evaluate Yourself

Check (✓) the category that best describes you as a speaker.

Category	Characteristics
❏ **AVOIDER**	An avoider does everything possible to escape from having to get in front of an audience. In some cases avoiders may seek careers that do not involve making presentations.
❏ **RESISTER**	A resister has fear when asked to speak. This fear may be strong. Resisters may not be able to avoid speaking as part of their job, but they never encourage it. When they do speak they do so with great reluctance and considerable pain.
❏ **ACCEPTER**	The accepter will give presentations as part of the job but doesn't seek those opportunities. Accepters occasionally give a presentation and feel as though they did a good job. They even find that once in a while they are quite persuasive, and enjoy speaking in front of a group.
❏ **SEEKER**	A seeker looks for opportunities to speak. The seeker understands that anxiety can be a stimulant which fuels enthusiasm during a presentation. Seekers work at building their professional communication skills and self-confidence by speaking often.

Assess Your Current Presentation Skills

To be a more effective presenter, it is useful to examine your present skills. The following evaluation can help determine the areas on which to focus to increase your competency. Please read the statement and then circle the number that best describes you. Then concentrate during the balance of this book on those items you marked 1, 2, or 3.

	Always				Never
1. I thoroughly analyze my audience.	5	4	3	2	1
2. I determine some basic objectives before planning a presentation.	5	4	3	2	1
3. I write down some main ideas first, in order to build a presentation around them.	5	4	3	2	1
4. I incorporate both a preview and review of the main ideas as my presentation is organized.	5	4	3	2	1
5. I develop an introduction that will catch the attention of my audience and still provide the necessary background information.	5	4	3	2	1
6. My conclusion refers back to the introduction and, if appropriate, contains a call-to-action statement.	5	4	3	2	1
7. The visual and graphics I use are carefully prepared, simple, easy to read, and have impact.	5	4	3	2	1
8. The number of visuals and graphics I use will enhance, not detract, from my presentation.	5	4	3	2	1
9. I use both energy and composure in delivering a presentation.	5	4	3	2	1
10. I ensure the benefits suggested to my audience are clear and compelling.	5	4	3	2	1
11. I communicate ideas with enthusiasm.	5	4	3	2	1
12. I rehearse so there is a minimum focus on notes and maximum attention paid to my audience.	5	4	3	2	1

13. My notes contain only "key words" so I avoid reading from a manuscript or technical paper.   5   4   3   2   1

14. My presentations are rehearsed standing up and using my visuals.   5   4   3   2   1

15. I prepare answers to anticipated questions, and practice responding to them.   5   4   3   2   1

16. I arrange seating (if appropriate) and check audio-visual equipment in advance of the presentation.   5   4   3   2   1

17. I maintain good eye contact with the audience at all times.   5   4   3   2   1

18. My gestures are natural and not constrained by anxiety.   5   4   3   2   1

19. My voice is strong and clear and is not a monotone.   5   4   3   2   1

Total score   _____

If you scored between 80–95, you are an accomplished speaker who simply needs to maintain basic skills through practice.

If your total score was between 60–80, you have the potential to become a highly effective presenter.

If your score was between 40 and 60, this book can help you significantly.

If you scored between 30 and 40, you should show dramatic improvement with practice.

If your total was below 30, roll up your sleeves and dig in. It may not be easy–but you can make excellent progress if you try.

At the conclusion of this program, take this evaluation again and compare your scores. You should be pleased with the progress you have made.

SET SOME GOALS

If your score on the previous page was:

90–95   You have the qualities of an excellent presenter.

70–89   You are above average but could improve in some areas.

Below 69   This program should help you.

What Goals Do You Want To Achieve?

Using the information from the self-evaluation form on pages 4 and 5, check (✔) those boxes that indicate goals that you would like to achieve:

I hope to:

❑ Understand the anxiety I feel before a presentation and learn how to use it constructively during my presentation.

❑ Learn how to organize my thoughts and data in a logical and concise manner.

❑ Develop the necessary skills to communicate enthusiasm about the ideas I present, and develop a more dynamic presentation style.

❑ Transform question-and-answer sessions into an enjoyable and productive part of the presentation process.

❑ Construct visual aids that have impact, and use them effectively during my presentation.

Dealing with Anxiety

Anxiety is a natural state that exists any time we are placed under stress. Giving a presentation will normally cause some stress. When this type of stress occurs, physiological changes take place that may cause symptoms such as a nervous stomach, sweating, tremors in the hands and legs, accelerated breathing, and/or increased heart rate.

Don't worry! If you have any of these symptoms before or during a presentation, you are normal. If none of these things happen, you are one in a million. Almost everyone experiences some stress before presentations, even when the task is something simple like, "tell the group something about yourself." The trick is to make your excess energy work for you.

When you learn to make stress work for you, it can be the fuel for a more enthusiastic and dynamic presentation. The next few pages will teach you how to recycle your stress in a positive form that will help you become a better presenter.

As someone once said, "The trick is to get those butterflies in your stomach to fly in one direction!"

Paul is an engineer with a large telecommunications company. In two weeks he has to deliver a major presentation to managers from several divisions in his company, on a project he is proposing. He knows his topic, but his audience will be examining his proposal very closely, and Paul is certain he will receive some very tough questions. Every time Paul thinks about planning what to say, he gets too nervous to begin work.

If Paul's problem of anxiety before a presentation sounds familiar, then the following may help.

Tips for Reducing Anxiety

1 Organize

Lack of organization is one of the major causes of anxiety. Later in this book you will learn a simple technique for organizing your presentation. Knowing that your thoughts are well organized will give you more confidence, which will allow you to focus energy into your presentation.

2 Visualize

Imagine walking into a room, being introduced, delivering your presentation with enthusiasm, fielding questions with confidence, and leaving the room knowing you did a great job. Mentally rehearse this sequence with all the details of your particular situation, and it will help you focus on what you need to do to be successful.

3 Practice

Many speakers rehearse a presentation mentally or with just their lips. Instead, you should practice standing up, as if an audience were in front of you, and use your visual aids (if you have them.) At least two dress rehearsals are recommended. If possible, have somebody critique the first one and/or have it videotaped. Watch the playback, listen to the critique, and incorporate any changes you feel are required before your final practice session. There is no better preparation than this.

Carol is an account executive with a software company. She has been asked to present the sales figures for her region at the company's national sales meeting. Her colleague Jack is finishing his remarks and in two minutes she will have to stand up and make her presentation. She is experiencing extreme anxiety at a time when she needs to be focused and collected.

Carol's situation is quite common. If you experience anxiety immediately before speaking, try some of the following exercises next time you're waiting for your turn to stand up and speak.

4 Breathe

When your muscles tighten and you feel nervous, you may not be breathing deeply enough. The first thing to do is to sit up, erect but relaxed, and inhale deeply a number of times.

5 Focus on relaxing

Instead of thinking about the tension—focus on relaxing. As you breathe, tell yourself on the inhale, "I am" and on the exhale, "relaxed." Try to clear your mind of everything except the repetition of the "I am-relaxed" statement and continue this exercise for several minutes.

6 Release tension

As tension increases and your muscles tighten, nervous energy can get locked into the limbs. This unreleased energy may cause your hands and legs to shake. Before standing up to give a presentation, it is a good idea to try to release some of this pent up tension by doing a simple, unobtrusive isometric exercise.

Starting with your toes and calf muscles, tighten your muscles up through your body finally making a fist (i.e., toes, feet calves, thighs, stomach, chest, shoulders, arms, and fingers). Immediately release all of the tension and take a deep breath. Repeat this exercise until you feel the tension start to drain away. Remember, this exercise is to be done quietly so that no one knows you're relaxing!

Andrew is an accountant with a major financial organization. When he gives presentations he gets very nervous. He sweats, his hands tremble, his voice becomes a monotone (and at times inaudible). He also fidgets with items, such as a pen, and looks at this notes or the overhead projector screen, not at his audience. He can barely wait to finish and return to his seat.

Andrew's plight is not uncommon. You may not have all of these symptoms, but you can probably relate to some of them. The following techniques will help you in situations where you get nervous while speaking.

7 Move

Speakers who stand in one spot and never gesture experience tension. In order to relax, you need to release tension by allowing your muscles to flex. If you find you are locking your arms in one position when you speak, then practice releasing them so that they do the same thing they would if you were in an animated one-on-one conversation. You can't gesture too much if it is natural.

Upper body movement is important, but moving with your feet can serve to release tension as well. You should be able to take a few steps, either side-to-side or toward the audience. When speaking from a lectern, you can move around the side of it for emphasis (if you have a moveable microphone). This movement will help release your tension and never fail to draw the audience into the presentation. If you can't move to the side of the lectern, an occasional half-step to one side will help loosen muscle tension.

8 Make eye contact with the audience

Give your presentation to one person at a time. Relate with your audience as individuals. Look in peoples' eyes as you speak. Connect with them. Make it personal and personable. The eye contact should help you relax because you become less isolated from the audience, and learn to react to their interest in you.

REVIEW CHECKLIST
DEALING WITH ANXIETY

Check (✓) those items you intend to practice and incorporate in the future presentations you make.

I plan to:

- ❑ Organize my material
- ❑ Visualize myself delivering a successful presentation
- ❑ Rehearse by standing up and using all of my visual aids
- ❑ Breathe deeply just prior to speaking and during my presentation
- ❑ Focus on relaxing with simple, unobtrusive isometric techniques
- ❑ Release my tension in a positive way by directing it to my audience
- ❑ Move when I speak to stay relaxed and natural
- ❑ Maintain good eye contact with my audience

Practice Makes Perfect!

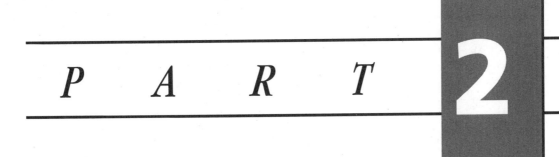

Planning Your Presentation

14

Personal Appearance

This section is not intended to provide specific fashion guidelines but rather some general considerations on your dress and appearance. In general, avoid excess. Keep patterns, accessories, and colors simple. You should be the focus, not what you are wearing.

There is a growing trend toward casual dress in the workplace. "Business casual" has replaced suits for both men and women in many environments. In terms of a presentation, who is in the audience will always determine how you should dress. When in doubt, dress up a bit.

For Women

1. Clothes should fit well, not too tight. Hem length should be decided upon by what works for you and what you will look like to those in the audience, especially if you are sitting up on a stage. Generally, longer sleeves are recommended to maintain a more business-like appearance.

2. Find two or three colors that work well with your complexion and hair color. You might wish to consult one of the many books on the subject or contact a "color consultant." You can then combine complimentary accessories with your basic outfits to provide variety. Find good fabrics and make sure that they don't make noise when you move! Generally, avoid very bright reds and oranges and blacks and whites since these colors are harsher and tend to draw attention away from the face.

3. Avoid jewelry that sparkles, dangles, or makes noise. More subtle accessories are called for when you are the presenter. Earrings, brooches, and bracelets that distract will annoy the audience and draw attention away from your presentation.

4. Makeup should be simple and compliment the wearer. Overdone makeup can become the focus of negative, and unwanted, attention. Makeup that is well done can control oily areas of the face that might reflect light, enhance natural features, and help you look more relaxed even in the most difficult presentation situations.

5. Hair, like other aspects of your appearance, should add to a positive overall impression of our appearance. While styles are highly individual, they should not be the dominant feature of the face.

For Men

1. Suits should be well tailored. For presentations, clothes that are checkered, brightly colored, or that clash will not reflect well on your image. Generally, dark blues, grays, and blacks in single or double-breasted classic styles are the safest bet. Depending on the audience, a sport coat and well-matched trousers may do.

2. Men's suit coats are designed to be buttoned whereas many women's coats are not. In a presentation, depending on the level of formality, you may wish to button the jacket, unbutton it, or take the coat off altogether.

3. Shirts should fit well and the color should not be too bright. If you are worried about perspiration showing, wear a cotton T-shirt and a white shirt. If going on TV, avoid white shirts, in favor of a light gray.

4. Ties can be used to compliment the color of your eyes and face. The traditional red "power tie" may not be the best color for you. Experiment a bit. The red tie causes the audience's eyes to focus first on the tie and not on you. Subtler colors may work better for you.

5. Shoes should be appropriate, comfortable, and well shined. Make sure that socks match, and that they cover any bare leg when you sit down.

6. Hair frames the face. It should be well groomed regardless of style. Beards should be well groomed also, and mustaches should be trimmed above the lip line.

And a word about glasses for both sexes...

The rule of thumb in presentations is to wear glasses if you need them to see the audience or read visuals, and so on. If you do need them, you might consider an anti-glare coating on the glasses. The reason for this is that the glass reflects light in the room and the audience will not be able to see your eyes. The coating eliminates glare and allows others to clearly see your eyes. Also, avoid tinted lenses since this will increase the audiences' difficulty in seeing your eyes.

Eight Steps to Preparing Your Presentation

Part of planning a presentation means that you must ask yourself why, not what. The "what" part will be answered when you begin to organize your thoughts. In the beginning, you should concern yourself with why you are giving a presentation to a particular audience. The answer to this question should help you plan your presentation.

For example, you have been asked to give a presentation to a group of managers in your company on next year's departmental budget. Don't start writing down what you expect to say. Instead, ask yourself what you want to accomplish with your presentation. What is your opinion about the topic? Will you be asking for a budget increase, presenting a plan to increase company revenue or simply asking the audience to consider a new idea? What's in it for the audience members if they do what you ask?

Can you imagine building a house without a set of plans? Before anyone can build a house, he or she needs plans to guide the purchase of the materials and to show how these materials will be used. In the same way, a plan for your presentation will make the actual work of putting it together much more efficient. However, before we plan the house we need to be clear about what the people are like who will be living in it, and what design elements will work best for them.

Step 1: Analyzing Your Audience

Put yourself in the shoes of the people who will be listening to your presentation. When analyzing your audience, you have five items to consider:

Needs

It is important to find out in advance of the presentation what the group thinks they need–this may be quite different from what you thought they needed. The speaker then must find a way to resolve the discrepancy. You can ask a representative of the audience about this, or, before you start the presentation, you can ask the audience, if appropriate, what they need to hear.

Attitude

How do they feel about the topic? Are they positive or negative on the subject? Or perhaps the group is mixed? Maybe certain sections of the presentation will generate strong feelings in either direction. What you uncover here must be factored into the structure and phrasing of the presentation.

Knowledge Level

All of us have our own area of specialization. Speakers must be careful not to use technical language, abbreviations, acronyms, buzz words, and so on that people in the audience might not understand. If in doubt, ask the audience if they are familiar with the terminology and define it if necessary.

Environment

Consider the room and general environment in which you will be speaking. Could seating, room size, equipment availability, and lighting effect your interaction with the audience? Environment can also be thought of in terms of the psychological environment. Is there anything going on with audience members that might effect their reception of you and your ideas? Psychological environment could be affected by recent good news/bad news (the company landed a huge contract or the company just announced some "downsizing").

Demographic Information

This may include the age, gender, race, religion, culture, and language of the audience members. Of these, culture and language present the greatest challenge to speakers. In delivering to international audiences it is a good idea to gain an understanding of any cultural differences that may effect the way in which you present. Also, you may need to understand the language level of your audience—some members may not be native speakers of the language you are using. Find out in advance if you need an interpreter.

AUDIENCE ANALYSIS WORKSHEET

This form should help you plan more efficiently for any presentation.

1. The specific needs of the audience members are:

   _____

   _____

2. Their attitude towards the topic is:

   _____

   _____

3. The knowledge level of the audience in relation to the subject matter is:

   _____

   _____

4. What are the physical or psychological environmental elements that might effect the audience:

   _____

   _____

5. The demographic factors in the audience that might impact your presentation are:

   _____

   _____

Step 2: Develop Position–Action–Benefit

Before developing the body of the presentation, and after doing a thorough audience analysis, clarify what you intend to do in the presentation by developing the following position, action, and benefit statements:

Position: This is a sentence that tells the audience what you personally think about the topic. It is your stance, your opinion, your thesis, your belief on the issue. It must be stated clearly and succinctly. It is important to put this information out to the audience at the start of the presentation; it tells the audience exactly where you stand so they won't be wondering what the presentation is all about (as many audiences do)!

Example: *"Our current computer system is outdated and is costing us too much money to maintain."*

Action: This is simply a statement of what you would like your audience to do, to believe, or to understand. There is a wide range of "actions" an audience might take. It might be that you want them to purchase a computer network system from your company. Or maybe you want them to know that when designing certain computer chips, experiments show that gallium arsinide works better than pure silicon. The action you ask them to take should be specific, achievable, and done within a specific time frame.

Example: *"We should allocate an additional $200,000 this budget period for a new system."*

Benefit: This tells the audience what is in it for them if they do what you ask. It could range from (using the example above) the new network saving time and money (resulting in less downtime) to gallium arsinide being the chip material of choice in heat-sensitive electronics.

Example: *"By doing so, we will work much more efficiently and save a tremendous amount of money."*

Step 3: Brainstorm Main Ideas

Using Post-It® notes, note cards, or a similar tool, brainstorm some possible main ideas for your presentation. Write one idea on each Post-It®. Let the ideas flow at this point; do not edit—that will come later. The strategy is to generate as many ideas as possible.

Once you have a large number of ideas, begin eliminating some. Try to end up with between two and five main ideas. This is a typical number for one presentation. If you have more than five ideas, you should reduce them by making some of them subpoints.

Problems with current system	**Capabilities of proposed system**	**Benefits of proposed system**

These three ideas are the general assertions you plan to make to your audience. Specific explanations, evidence, and benefits will become your subpoints.

Step 4: State the Subpoints

Once you have the main points of your presentation, it is time to develop supporting ideas. These may consist of facts, data, references, stories, analogies, or other forms of evidence that support your main ideas as shown in the example. Using the information you have gathered, build a logical flow in your presentation.

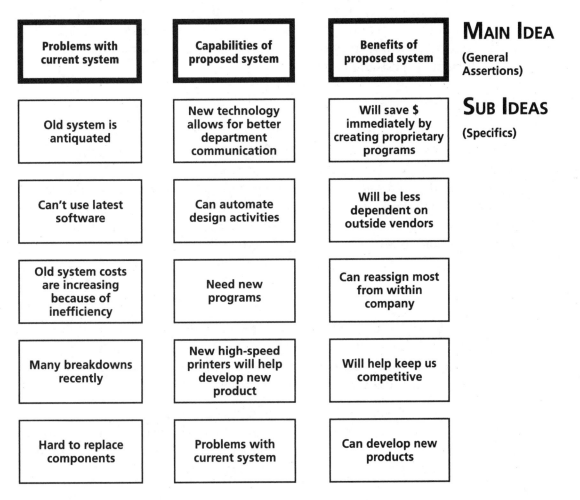

			MAIN IDEA (General Assertions)
Problems with current system	**Capabilities of proposed system**	**Benefits of proposed system**	
Old system is antiquated	New technology allows for better department communication	Will save $ immediately by creating proprietary programs	**SUB IDEAS** (Specifics)
Can't use latest software	Can automate design activities	Will be less dependent on outside vendors	
Old system costs are increasing because of inefficiency	Need new programs	Can reassign most from within company	
Many breakdowns recently	New high-speed printers will help develop new product	Will help keep us competitive	
Hard to replace components	Problems with current system	Can develop new products	

You may have more or fewer subpoints in your presentation. Once you have completed this procedure, rearrange your Post-its® to best suit your needs. Try different arrangements to see what will work best. Always keep your position, action, benefits, and audience in mind.

Step 5: Develop Introductions and Conclusions

The easiest way to open and close a presentation is simply to use your three-sentence Position, Action, and Benefit statement. This method for entry and exit works for 90% of business and technical presentations. However, there are times when a more formal introduction and conclusion are called for. However, keep in mind that the Position, Action, Benefit statement must immediately follow, and precede, the formal introductory device. Below you will find some common, and powerful, formal openers and closers:

Anecdote

An anecdote is a short story used to help illustrate a point. It is sometimes humorous but not always. An example might be something like this: "My son came to me the other day and said, 'Dad, if you raise my allowance by $2.00 I'll mow the lawn twice each week. For another 10% you will get the best looking lawn in the neighborhood.' In the same way, if we raise salaries for our production workers 10%, we should expect to increase productivity."

Humor

Humor is a great way to break the ice. But beware! Humor must be linked to the speaker, topic, audience, or the occasion. Also, never tell a joke that has do with sex, race, religion, or any other personal topic. If you ask yourself, "Should I tell that joke?"—don't! Be conservative with your use of humor.

There is nothing worse than a joke used in an introduction that has no connection to the speech (i.e., "Did you hear about the duck who walked into the store, ordered a lot of items, and asked it all to be put on his bill? Well, today I would like to talk about networking solutions.") Nothing is more embarrassing than a joke that falls flat.

Involving Question

There are two ways to do this. First, you can ask an open-ended question—but beware, someone might yell out the wrong answer or crack a joke at your expense. The second way, and the safer of the two, is to ask for a show of hands. It is no guarantee that you won't get heckled but generally audiences will respond the way you request them to.

Rhetorical Question

A rhetorical question is a question with an obvious answer. An example is, "How many people here want bigger research grants?" This device is an excellent way to get the audience's attention.

Shocking Statement

A statement such as, "Last year enough people died in automobile accidents to fill every seat in the local university's football stadium. This is why I am going to convince you to wear seatbelts." This type of statement will help capture your audience's attention.

Quotation

You may wish to begin your presentation with a brief quotation. Quotations should be limited to a sentence or two and the source of the quotation should always be given. It is OK to read a quotation directly since you want it to be accurate. Avoid memorizing all but the simplest or well-known quotes. You may wish to paraphrase a famous quote, possible something like, "To paraphrase Mark Twain, 'Everyone complains about the computer system but no one does anything about it!'"

A Final Word About Introductions and Conclusions

The position, action, and benefit must be clearly restated in the close of the presentation. Many speakers finish on the last main idea and fail to summarize and solidly conclude the presentation. The Position, Action, Benefit is the perfect way to do it. If you used a formal opener, such as an anecdote, or rhetorical question, then a restatement of that should follow the position, action, and benefit.

Introductions and conclusions put the head and tail on the body of your presentation. If they are missing, or not fully developed, you don't have a complete presentation and it will be evident to the audience.

Step 6: Formulate the Main Idea Preview/Review Sentence

Have you ever heard the saying:

> *"Tell them what you're going to tell them—*
>
> *Tell them—*
>
> *Then tell them what you told them!"*

In other words, preview and review the main points in your presentation. This should immediately follow, and precede respectively, the opening and closing of your presentation. This can be accomplished very easily by using a main idea preview sentence and a main idea review sentence. Going back to the three main points in our example it would sound something like this:

> *"Today I will talk about the problems with our current system, the capabilities of the new system I am proposing, and the benefits of installing it."*

Deliver Your Presentation in the Following Sequence

1. Introduction (Position, Action, Benefit)

2. Preview sentence (tell them what you're going to tell them)

3. Main ideas and sub ideas (tell them)

4. Review sentence (tell them what you told them)

5. Conclusion (Restate: Position, Action, Benefit)

Step 7: Develop Slides or other Visual Aids[*]

Once your organizational pattern has been established, you need to decide if and where you are going to use visual aids. Guidelines for developing and using visuals in a presentation are discussed later (beginning on page 34). For now it is important only that you determine how they will fit into your plan.

For example, in our sample presentation developed on page 23, the third subpoint under the first main idea, states that the old system is costing the company money because of inefficiency. This point could be illustrated with a graph, or similar visual, showing the cost of the computer over the past three years vs. the savings of a new system during the same time span.

---

[*] *In this book, the term "slides" is used to describe overhead transparencies and computer-projected graphics.*

Step 8: Develop Handouts

Now you can decide what handouts (if any) would add to your presentation.

Three major uses of handouts:

1. **To reinforce important information.**

2. **To summarize action items for the audience to follow up on.**

3. **To supply supporting data you don't want cluttering your visual aids.**

Once you have decided what handouts would be beneficial, you must then decide when you are going to hand them out. There are three alternatives.

Before the Presentation

This is the preferred method in business presentations. Typically, copies of the slides are distributed. You may choose to use the "Speaker Note" function in Microsoft® Power Point® so you can put narrative explanation on the page with the slide copy.

The main problem with this is that your audience may wish to satisfy their curiosity about the contents of your handout as you are speaking. When people are reading, they are not listening. One way to deal with this problem is to have the handout in place when the audience enters to room. This will allow them to read it before you begin speaking. In addition, you can explain the handout before actually starting the presentation, satisfying their curiosity about its contents.

During the Presentation

This must be used carefully. Handouts during a presentation must be disbursed quickly and be relevant to the point you are making. Otherwise they will be a distraction, not an aid.

At the End of the Presentation

During your presentation you can inform the audience that they will receive a handout covering such and such points at the end your presentation. This will allow them to avoid having to take unnecessary notes. However, whether or not you use this technique depends on your audience analysis. If the audience is accustomed to receiving handouts with presentations, or if it would be useful for them to follow the presentation with the data before them, you might not want to withhold them. If handouts—such as glossy photos, marketing brochures—are going to distract from your oral presentation and not add substantially to the message, hold them back.

REVIEW CHECKLIST
PLANNING AND ORGANIZING
YOUR PRESENTATION

Use this sheet to help prepare your next presentation.

For my presentation I have:

❑ Analyzed the Audience

❑ Developed Position, Action, Benefit Statements

❑ Brainstormed Main Ideas

❑ Stated Subpoints

❑ Developed Introduction and Conclusion

❑ Formulated the Main Idea Preview/Review Sentence

❑ Developed Slides and Visuals

❑ Developed Handouts

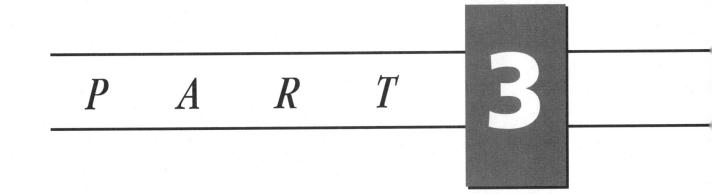

PART 3

Slides and Other Visual Aids

Developing and Using Visuals

In this section you will learn how to prepare and use slides and other visual aids in your presentation. Most presentations in the business and technical world use either overhead transparencies or, more and more frequently, computer projected slides. So, we will focus on their use. However, tips on using flip charts, whiteboards, and other media are also covered in this section.

Use slides or visuals when you need to:	Do not use slides or visuals to:
1. Focus the audience's attention 2. Reinforce your verbal message (but not repeat it verbatim!) 3. Stimulate interest 4. Illustrate factors that are hard to visualize	1. Impress your audience with overwhelming detail or animation 2. Avoid interaction with your audience 3. Make more than one main point per slide 4. Present simple ideas that are easily stated orally

10 Tips for Planning Successful Slides and Visuals

When considering what type of visual representation to use for your data or ideas, here are some rules of thumb to consider:

1 Use slides sparingly.

One of the biggest problems in technical presentations is the overuse of slides. A useful rule of thumb is one slide for every two minutes of presentation time.

2 Make slides pictorial.

Graphs, pictures of equipment, flow charts, etc., all give the viewer an insight that would otherwise require many words or columns of numbers.

3 Present one key point per slide.

Keep the focus of the slide simple and clear. Presenting more than one main idea per slide can seriously detract from the impact.

4 Make text and numbers legible.

Minimum font size for most room set-ups is 20 pt. Can the audience read everything? If not, be prepared to provide additional explanation in handout material or highlight the areas of the chart where you want the audience to focus.

5 Use color carefully.

Use no more than three or four colors per slide to avoid a cluttered look. The colors used should contrast with each other to provide maximum visibility—for example, a dark blue background with light yellow letters or numbers.

6 **Make visuals big enough to see.**
Walk to the last row where people will be sitting and make sure that everything on the slide can be seen clearly.

7 **Graph data.**
Whenever possible avoid tabular data in favor of graphs. Graphs allow the viewer to picture the information and data in a way that numbers alone can't. Information on how to graph data is provided on the following pages.

8 **Make pictures and diagrams easy to see.**
Too often pictures and diagrams are difficult to see from a distance. The best way to ascertain this is to view it from the back of the room. Make sure that labels inside the diagrams are legible from the back row also.

9 **Avoid unnecessary slides.**
If something can be stated simply and orally, such as the title of a presentation, there is no need for a slide.

10 **Use builds and animation very sparingly.**
They can interfere with the content of your message.

Content Guidelines

Number Charts

Use a maximum of 25–35 numbers per visual aid. One number may contain many digits, so use your best judgment. The general rule of thumb is to put raw data into the handout material or on backup slides. Data charts should only contain bottom line information, conclusions, and final results.

AVOID THIS

Monthly Cumulative Totals

	Accepts	Volume	Returns	Amount
	179.880	423.3660	967	334.07
	128.864	345.7670	860	287.74
	34.221	678.4440	733	982.21
	129.775	654.9980	1887	658.89
	378.664	739.6000	431	295.58
	194.775	187.4659	223	295.50
	198.856	189.9570	582	377.89
	746.599	879.9560	334	867.73
	286.675	385.7689	233	286.57
	196.999	285.8678	188	296.97
	185.868	286.8786	299	185.90
Totals	2661.767	5058.3140	6737	4869.13

In this case, only the totals line is essential—the rest of the information could be put in a handout.

THIS IS BETTER

Monthly Cumulative Totals

Accepts	Volume	Returns	Amounts
2661	5058	6737	4869

Avoid "Data Dump." Crowding your presentation with too many slides and/or too much information will reduce their effectiveness and impact. Usually, the fewer, the better!

Text Charts

For word slides–use the 5 x 5 rule (five lines with a maximum of five words per line). This will result in no more than 25 words in the body of the slide (excluding the title). If you need more room, (as in the example below), use more lines, but fewer words. There is no need to repeat every word in your presentation. You simply want to reinforce your main ideas for the audience.

AVOID THIS

How to Organize Your Presentation

It is a good idea to start by analyzing your audience. Once this is done you need to formulate a Position, Action, Benefit statement. You must complete these steps before you separately brainstorm the main ideas and the subpoints of your presentation. You then gather factual information and prepare a blueprint of your presentation. Also prepare any slides, handouts, and notes you will need. And don't forget to practice!

This slide is more effective when it is set up as follows:

THIS IS BETTER

HOW TO ORGANIZE YOUR PRESENTATION

- **Develop Position, Action, Benefit**

- **Brainstorm Main Ideas and Subpoints**

- **Develop Introduction and Conclusion**

- **State Main Idea Preview/Review Sentence**

- **Develop Visuals, Handouts, and Notes**

Stating information clearly and concisely on your slides makes it easier for the audience to retain information.

Types of Charts and Graphs

Following are several examples of how different types of information can be effectively presented using slides.

Percent

Shows a comparison as a percentage of the whole. Usually uses the pie chart or map chart.

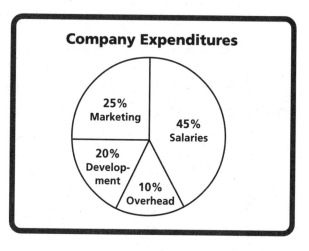

Parts

Shows how items compare in rank. Usually a bar (horizontal lines) or column chart (vertical lines).

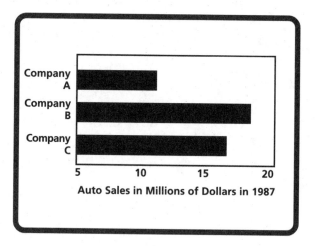

Time

Shows changes over a period of time. Column or line charts are most typical.

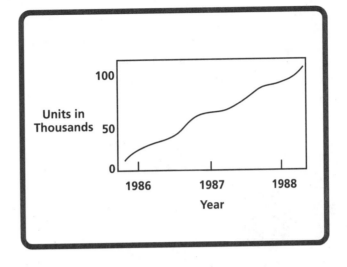

Frequency

Shows the number of items in different numerical ranges. Column and line charts are also used here.

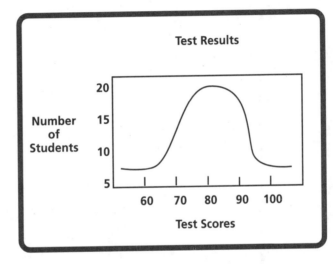

Correlation

Shows the relationship between variables. Bar charts and dot charts are used to illustrate correlation.

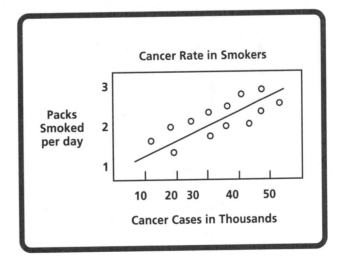

Tip: *When constructing visuals or graphics, employ the K.I.S.S. principle–*
Keep It Short and Simple! Don't overload slides with too much data.
When you do, your audience will quickly lose interest or get lost.

Avoid slides like this one.

AVOID THIS

$$\left[1 - \frac{u}{u^*}\right] \mathbf{Q}_{d-1}\left[\mathbf{V}_0^{[0]}(u^*), \mathbf{V}_0^{[1]}(u^*), \ldots, \mathbf{V}_0^{[d-1]}(u^*); 0, u^*; \frac{u}{u^*}\right]$$

$$+ \frac{u}{u^*}\left[u^* \mathbf{Q}_{d-1}\left[\mathbf{V}_1^{[0]}(u^*), \mathbf{V}_1^{[1]}(u^*), \ldots, \mathbf{V}_1^{[d-1]}(u^*); 0, u^*; \frac{u}{u^*}\right]\right.$$

$$\left. + (1 - u^*) \mathbf{Q}_{d-1}\left[\mathbf{V}_0^{[0]}(u^*), \mathbf{V}_0^{[1]}(u^*), \ldots, \mathbf{V}_0^{[d-1]}(u^*); 0, u^*; \frac{u}{u^*}\right]\right]$$

Regrouping, we have

$$\left[1 - \frac{u}{u^*}\right] \mathbf{Q}_{d-1}\left[\mathbf{V}_0^{[0]}(u^*), \mathbf{V}_0^{[1]}(u^*), \ldots, \mathbf{V}_0^{[d-1]}(u^*); 0, u^*; \frac{u}{u^*}\right]$$

$$+ \frac{u}{u^*} \mathbf{Q}_{d-1}\left[(1 - u^*) \mathbf{V}_0^{[0]} + u^* \mathbf{V}_1^{[0]}(u^*),\right.$$

$$(1 - u^*) \mathbf{V}_0^{[1]} + u^* \mathbf{V}_1^{[1]}(u^*), \ldots,$$

$$\left. (1 - u^*) \mathbf{V}_0^{[d-1]} + u^* \mathbf{V}_1^{[d-1]}(u^*); 0, u^*; \frac{u}{u^*}\right]$$

By definition (10.12) of $\mathbf{V}_i^{[r]}(u^*)$, this becomes

$$\left[1 - \frac{u}{u^*}\right] \mathbf{Q}_{d-1}\left[\mathbf{V}_0^{[0]}(u^*), \mathbf{V}_0^{[1]}(u^*), \ldots, \mathbf{V}_0^{[d-1]}(u^*); 0, u^*; \frac{u}{u^*}\right]$$

$$+ \frac{u}{u^*} \mathbf{Q}_{d-1}\left[\mathbf{V}_0^{[1]}(u^*), \mathbf{V}_0^{[2]}(u^*), \ldots, \mathbf{V}_0^{[d]}(u^*); 0, u^*; \frac{u}{u^*}\right]$$

But from (10.6), this is just

$$\mathbf{Q}_d\left[\mathbf{V}_0^{[0]}(u^*), \mathbf{V}_0^{[1]}(u^*), \ldots, \mathbf{V}_0^{[d]}(u^*); 0, u^*; \frac{u}{u^*}\right]$$

Simplify the slide and focus audience attention where you want it.

Using Color

With the ready availability of presentation software, color printers, and computer projectors, using color in slides is now quite easy. Presentation software programs all provide ready-made templates and color schemes. Or, your company or organization may have a color scheme or template for you to follow. If you are choosing from those available in presentation software usually the simpler designs are preferable.

Basic principles for using color in slides:

1. Keep a consistent theme or template throughout the presentation.

2. Generally, use a clear background for overheads and a color background for computer projected slides.

3. Use high contrast to increase legibility (e.g., black text on clear and yellow on dark blue).

4. Colors should not clash—they should have a high degree of harmony.

5. Avoid clutter by using no more than three or four colors.

Developing Titles

There are three types of titles for your visual aids. The assertive title is usually preferred.

Topic Title

Used when it is not necessary to convey a specific message but only to provide information or raw data, as in the example to the right.

> **SALES FIGURES**

Thematic Title

Used to tell the audience what information they should draw from the data presented. An example would be:

> **SALES IN 1987 WERE UP 22% OF 1986**

Assertive Title

Used when you want to give the audience your opinion about what conclusion they should draw from the data.

> **WE SHOULD FOCUS OUR SALES EFFORT IN THE WESTERN U.S.**

Tip: *Make your presentation people-centered, not media-centered. Avoid using too many slides and putting too much information on them. While you may need to use slides to present your data, remember that building rapport and interacting with your audience is critical. Slides alone cannot make a presentation interesting—your enthusiasm and delivery is the key to making a presentation lively.*

Visualizing Ideas

Use the following form to help you plan and visualize the slides you would like to use in a presentation. The first one is done for you as an example:

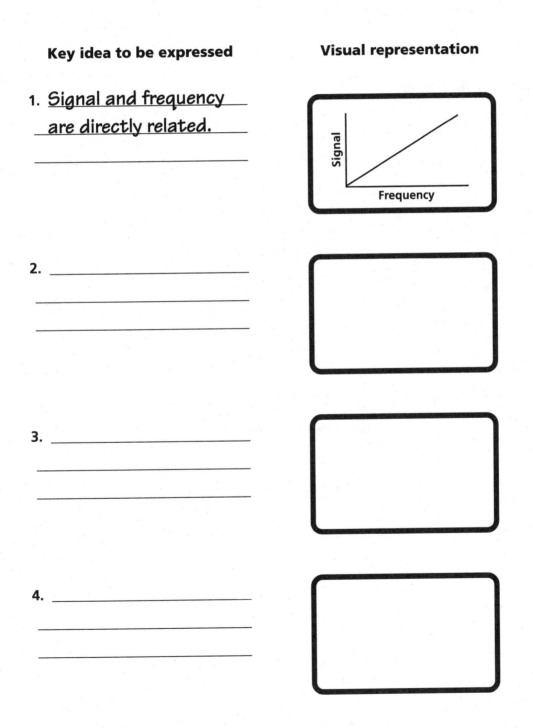

Key idea to be expressed

Visual representation

1. <u>Signal and frequency</u>
   <u>are directly related.</u>

2.

3.

4.

Revelation and "Build" Slides

Covering part of an overhead transparency and revealing the contents by sliding the cover down is often used to control the audience's attention. Not surprisingly, most audiences do not appreciate this technique! So, it is not recommended.

For computer-projected slides, you can "build" complicated information using the animation feature of the software. Just be careful about overusing this technique.

When using "build" slides:

- Use a consistent build direction throughout the presentation, i.e., all from the left or all from the top.

- Don't use a build on every single bullet point—it gets too repetitious.

- Build to illustrate a process or sequence. For example, don't build the following information, just put the whole slide up:

Build a slide like this one that illustrates a process:

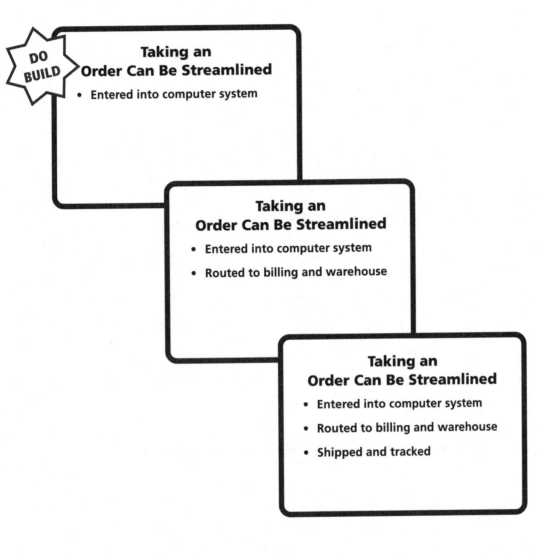

Directing Your Audience's Focus

Learn to direct the audience's focus where you want it. When you use slides, the audience's focus is divided. To win them back, you will need to redirect their focus. This is usually done by "blacking out" the slides, as explained below, and taking a step or two towards the audience.

Tip: *Decide in advance where the audience should focus. Do you want the focus divided between you and the visuals, or do you need their undivided attention?*

CHECKLIST FOR
KEEPING YOUR AUDIENCE FOCUSED

Place a check (✓) next to the techniques that you plan to use in your presentation.

I plan to:

❑ When appropriate, temporarily black out the screen to focus the audience's attention on myself. (In Microsoft® Power Point® this is accomplished by hitting the "B" key while in Slide Show.)

❑ Shut off the overhead projector when giving a lengthy explanation and there is no need for the audience to watch the screen. I won't click the machine on and off frequently, but also I won't leave it on so long that they focus on the transparency and not on me.

❑ Turn a flip chart page when I have finished referring to it. When preparing flip charts in advance, I will leave three blank pages between each prepared sheet so my next page won't show until I'm ready for it.

❑ Erase the whiteboard when I am finished making a point, for the reasons outlined above. Any information noted by the audience and no longer needed for future reference can be erased.

❑ Show or demonstrate an object at the appropriate point and then cover it up when it is no longer in use. If the object remains visible, most people will continue looking out of curiosity and may miss some of my presentation.

❑ Avoid passing objects around the audience since this is very distracting. Instead, I will walk into the audience and show the object to everyone briefly and, then, make it available at the end of the session.

Directing Your Audience's Focus (CONTINUED)

Placement of Equipment

When using a computer projector or overhead it should add, not detract, from your presentation. This can be accomplished by placing the screen (or flip chart) at a 45-degree angle and slightly to one side of the center of the room. In this way a presenter can occupy the central position and more easily focus the audience's attention on the explanation of the data being displayed.

Figure 1 shows how a room can be set up to maximize audience focus on the speaker. Figure 2 shows the room set up where the speaker is competing for attention with the visuals.

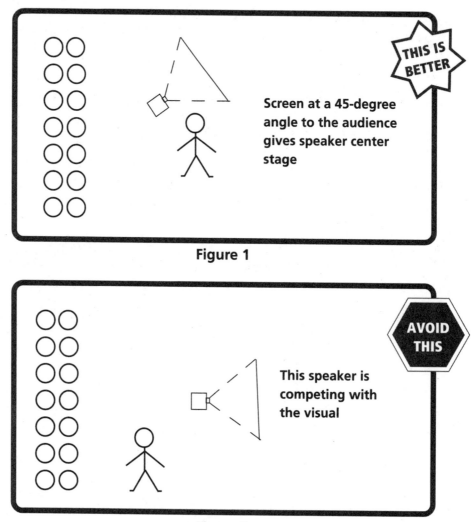

THIS IS BETTER

Screen at a 45-degree angle to the audience gives speaker center stage

Figure 1

AVOID THIS

This speaker is competing with the visual

Figure 2

Where and How to Stand

One major problem when using visual aids is that speakers often give their presentation to the visuals and not to the audience. This problem can be easily corrected if the speaker remembers to keep shoulder orientation toward the audience at all times as illustrated in Figure 1. Figure 2 shows what happens when your shoulders turn toward the visuals.

Figure 1

Figure 2

Tips on Using a Pointer

Laser pointers are needed only rarely, and yet they tend to be overused. When you do need to use one, remember:

➤ Don't try to point with it if your hand is trembling. Instead, briefly circle the part of the graph or drawing you want the audience to focus on, and then put the pointer down.

➤ Pointers are not needed on text slides since you can refer to each point by an item or number. Pointers should only be used to make a quick visual reference on a graphic slide, or to trace the relationship of data on a graph.

➤ Keep your body oriented toward the audience. Do not cross your arm over your body to refer to something on the screen. Instead, hold the pointer in the hand closest to the screen.

➤ If you are using an overhead projector don't leave a pen, pencil, or other type of pointer on top of the machine as a pointer. This can be very distracting.

Tip: *Do not speak until you have eye contact with your audience! Look at the screen momentarily to recall the point you want to make and then turn to the audience and deliver it. If you must write something on the flip chart, overhead, or whiteboard, stop talking while you write.*

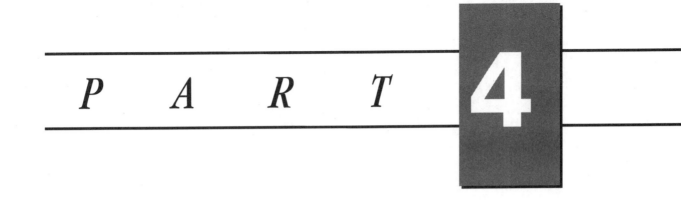

New Technology for Presentations

Computer Technology

The advances in computer technology have led to tremendous leaps in presentation technology. You can easily merge photos, sound, and video into a presentation on your computer and project it directly from the computer onto a screen. It won't be long before some presentations will be made using virtual reality! Here is a brief overview of current technology for creating slides and graphics.

Computers

Regardless of the type of system, current technology demands an increasing amount of available memory. If you are considering purchasing a laptop, or desktop system, it would probably be wise to get the most RAM you can. Depending on your requirements you might also need a video capture card.

Scanners

Scanners allow you to take a photo or document, digitize it, and bring it into the computer so that it can be changed or otherwise manipulated. Depending on the software that is being used, scanned photos can be placed in documents, on-screen presentations, or in visual aids. Scanners are priced about the same as printers and produce images of outstanding quality.

Computer Projectors

These devices have advanced to the stage where they can be used in a fully lit room. You usually need a machine that will produce at least 1000 lumens (the measurement of brightness). The costs of these machines are still high, but they are coming down in price and are increasingly portable.

Using Presentation Software

The effective use of visuals can play an important role in successful presentations. Slides, for example, can enhance a speaker's impact if they are thoughtfully created and skillfully used. Often, however, slides are included in ways that add little or actually detract from a presentation.

When Slides Help

Slides can add significant improvements to the persuasiveness of a presentation. They are especially effective for:

➤ Focusing your audience's attention

➤ Stimulating interest

➤ Reinforcing key ideas or data

➤ Illustrating hard-to-understand points

➤ Increasing audience retention of your content

Management Information Systems Research Center, School of Management, University of Minnesota, Persuasion and the Role of Visual Presentation Support: The UM/3M Study (Minneapolis: University of Minnesota, 1986).

When They Don't

Unfortunately, many speakers use slides in ways that reduce, rather than enhance, their presentation's impact on the audience. Slides will detract from your presentation if:

> ➤ Used primarily to avoid audience interaction

> ➤ They contain overwhelming amounts of detail

> ➤ Slide content and/or sequencing contains too many points or no point at all

> ➤ The speaker reads the slides rather than uses them as supporting material

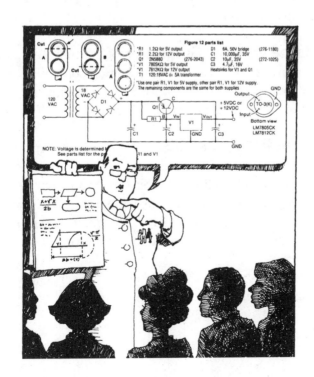

15 Tips for Creating Better Slides with Presentation Software

1 **Allow an average of two minutes per slide.** Use this rule of thumb to calculate the approximate number of slides you should use for your presentation. If your presentation includes complex diagrams or explanations, allow even more time per slide.

2 **Put your titles to work.** Whenever possible, the title of a slide should state the conclusion you want the audience to reach or the action you want people to take.

3 **Use the "5 x 5" guideline** for bullet-point slides. Limit the content of each slide to a maximum of five bullet points (including any subpoints) and a maximum of five words per bullet. Keep the grammar and style of bullet points consistent, and use a parallel structure for each point on a slide.

4 **Use phrases and key words** that quickly communicate the essence of each point. Carefully choose your words for each slide. If lengthy explanations, long sentences, and/or detailed descriptions are necessary, keep those for your handouts. For bullet points, avoid using full sentences.

5 **Capitalize only the first letter** of the first word and the first letter of proper nouns. Although some people like the look, capitalizing the first letter of every word in bullet points can cause slides to look busy, making them more difficult to read.

6 **Don't "build" every slide.** Audiences get weary of such repetition. The practice of revealing bullet points one at a time (the "build" technique) works well if not overdone. You can even "gray-out" points as you finish discussing them so the next point built on the slide will stand out more brightly. Also, avoid mixing different kinds of transition effects in the same presentation.

7 **Number every slide.** This can help viewers catch up if they join the presentation late or if they lose the thread of the discussion.

8 **Adhere to color scheme or style guidelines** used in your company. If you have freedom of choice for computer-projected slides, use dark colors for backgrounds or objects (like boxes, circles, lines, etc.) and light colors for text. For computer images projected to large audiences, information that is white or yellow on dark blue will be easier to read than the reverse.

9 **Consider using sans serif fonts** (fonts without strokes or "feet" at the ends of the letters), as some people find them easier and faster to read when projected from a slide. Arial and Helvetica are sans serif fonts. When projecting your presentation for a large audience, a sans serif font might improve readability, particularly for people in the back of the room.

10 **Use a 24 point font size** at the *minimum*, unless the audience is a small one. Do not expect your audience to be able to read a font smaller than 20 points.

11 **Pictures, photographs, and video clips** can break the monotony of slide after slide of bullet points. However, it is important to keep drawings and diagrams simple and to the point.

12 **Use clip art sparingly** and preferably not at all. Some companies have even banned the use of clip art!

13 **Animating drawings** (by building a slide in steps) is one of the simplest ways to keep an audience's attention. Just don't overdo it. While animation can help explain the flow of a complex process, too much animation keeps your audience waiting for the next visual trick, rather than paying attention to what you are saying.

14 **Have backups.** If you are not sure that you will be able to project your presentation from your laptop computer, have a version printed on overhead transparencies as a backup.

15 **Remember** the slides are not the messenger (*you* are). Your slides are just a communication aid.

Teleconferencing and Videoconferencing

In today's global business environment, people from different parts of the city, country, or world may be working "together" on the same project. It is not always practical or possible for these people to meet in person to resolve issues, and plan and coordinate details. A letter or memo, even if sent by fax, does not provide the opportunity for immediate interaction and feedback.

The following information will help you make "the next best thing"–telephone and videoconferencing–as effective as possible.

Advantages and Disadvantages

It helps to acknowledge in advance that a conference call, or even a videoconference, is not quite the same as a face-to-face meeting. Acknowledging the limitations and building on the strengths can help those involved use the tools most effectively.

WHAT ARE THE DISADVANTAGES?

Conference Calls:

➤ Participants' attention wanders because there is no visual element.

➤ The voice is the only "involvement" technique–there's no opportunity for non-verbal communication.

➤ "Speaker phone" syndrome–you're never sure who is really listening!

➤ Poor phone etiquette–people are impolite because they feel somewhat invisible.

Videoconferences:

➤ Equipment is not used to the best advantage. If the camera is pre-set on wide-angle, participants have difficulty focusing on who is actually speaking.

➤ Unrealistic expectations of clear communications. Voice activated microphones can make two-way communication awkward.

WHAT ARE THE ADVANTAGES?

The advantages for both conference calls and videoconferencing are very similar:

➤ **Cost savings:** Many, many thousands of dollars in travel costs can be saved. Business travel is a very expensive proposition when you take into account not only airfare, hotel, and meals, but also time away from the principal place of work.

➤ **Time savings:** A conference call is often taken right at your work station. A videoconference session is held at your principal place of employment, and time away from your desk is minimized. Time limitations, particularly on videoconferencing equipment, make it essential to keep the meeting moving along in a timely fashion, whereas face-to-face meetings can drag on.

➤ **Teamwork:** While budgets and time may allow for only one or two people to travel to another site, in a conference call or videoconference, more people can be involved. Information can be conveyed and clarified on the spot. Conferences can be held more frequently because the cost and time factors are greatly reduced.

Get Ready, Get Set, Go!

The following suggestions for before, during, and after a conference will help you make the most of the tools available. As with "live presentations," the more you practice, the easier it will become. Evaluate and modify your style until you find what works most effectively for your group.

Before:

Analyze the audience.

Sound familiar? Because you have acknowledged the limitations of conference calls and videoconferences, you need to build a very strong presentation. Talk to people at each site in advance to make sure you are giving them the information they need.

Develop a plan.

It is even more important in conference sessions to be extremely well organized. Review the section on organizing a presentation. Develop a position-action-benefit statement and key ideas you want to cover.

Send information out in advance.

Make sure all participants have a copy of the agenda, as well as copies of any visual aids you may be using. (Hint: if participants have a copy of an effective visual aid, it will help them to retain the information being discussed). Again, Keep It Short and Simple.

Make assignments in advance.

If participants know what they will be expected to contribute and prepare in advance, the conference will be much more effective.

Be aware of the limitations.

You can work with them. Keep the presentation lively and to the point. Do not get bogged down in endless detail if it can be avoided— provide the raw data, details, etc. in a separate handout packet.

Develop some ground rules in advance.

This will help govern question-and-answer techniques, interruptions, and etiquette for the conference.

SPECIFICALLY FOR VIDEOCONFERENCES

1. Familiarize yourself and your group with the equipment in advance. It would be helpful to have a short orientation, even if you have used the equipment before, so that you can familiarize yourself with the controls, how to zoom in, pan, sweep from left to right, where to position the overheads, and so on.

2. Arrange for someone other than the meeting facilitator to handle the equipment. Operating the camera and other equipment while participating in the meeting is difficult. Some facilities have a person on site who handles the equipment. If you aren't so lucky, ask for a volunteer!

During:

1 **Remember the power of an attention-grabbing introduction.**

Use your position-action-benefit statement. After you get the attention of your audience, review the agenda and the time schedule, and set any ground rules that may be necessary. Review the procedure for acknowledging and dealing with questions. However you set it up, remember that the ground rules need to be clear to everyone before you begin.

2 **Stick with the agenda you have designed.**

Your agenda needs to be flexible enough to allow time for feedback, but as in a live presentation, some lengthy discussions may have to be taken "off line." Remember the importance of an introduction and conclusion, as well as the preview and review.

3 **Use your voice!**

In a telephone conference, it is the only tool you have, and even in a videoconference, it is essential to keep your voice strong and engaging. Avoid a monotone, and please, please do not read. Talk.

4 **Take the temperature of the group periodically.**

In other words, build time into the agenda to hear from each site and clarify any misinformation. When communicating electronically the chances for mistakes in understanding multiply.

5 **Allow time for feedback.**

Reinforce commitment to action items at the review stage of the conference call.

SPECIFICALLY FOR
VIDEOCONFERENCES

1. Be aware of your body! Remember that others can see you, even if you are not the one talking. If your facility has a third monitor that allows you to preview what you will look like on screen, take advantage of it.

2. Avoid any side conversations. Because the systems are voice-activated, the picture starts to break up and re-focus on another location when it picks up a voice. If you need to have a side discussion, use the mute button.

3. Manage audience focus. Keep the presentation lively and use the equipment to its best advantage. Judiciously use the zoom to focus on the person speaking. When using visual aids, remember that the graphics need to be bold, simple, and to the point, just as they would in a "live" presentation. Avoid data dump; crowded or poorly designed visual aids are even more difficult to read from a camera than they are in person.

After:

Follow up! Make sure that copies of the minutes or action items are sent in a timely fashion. Talk to people at the other sites and get their feedback as to how the conference could have been made more effective. Establish a system to check on action items before the next conference.

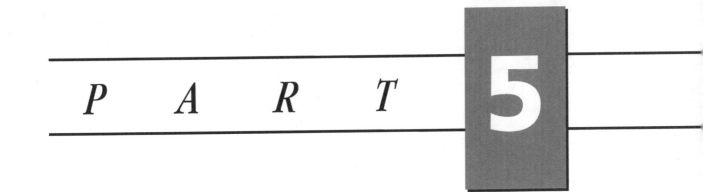

Preparing Your Presentation

Controlling the Presentation Environment

A few minutes of planning, checking equipment, and arranging seating can prevent disasters. Presenters can usually exercise a degree of control over their speaking environment.

Ed worked all week preparing for his quarterly presentation. He has rehearsed (standing up and using his slides) and feels prepared and confident. The morning of his presentation he arrives early to go over his material one final time.

As he enters the meeting room for his presentation, Ed notices his manager and his department head in the audience. He is anxious but knows he is prepared. Ed begins his presentation and then moves to the overhead projector to show his first transparency. He flips the switch and nothing happens. He notices the unit is plugged in. Next, he checks the bulb only to find it's burned out. Ed knows that most overhead projectors have spare bulbs, but when he looks for it he realizes someone did not bother to replace it. It takes him 20 minutes to track down a new bulb.

This situation could have been avoided if Ed had checked the projector in advance.

Items to think about before your presentation

✔ **Computer Hardware and Software**

Always check hardware and software immediately before the presentation to make sure all systems are functioning. Have a backup plan in mind should you have a breakdown—remember Murphy's Law.

✔ **Overhead Projector**

Is the bulb working and is a spare bulb available? Is the projection glass clean? Do you need extra transparencies and projectable pens to create overlays?

✔ **Flip Chart**

Is there enough paper? Do you have a supply of marking pens? Have you checked to make sure the pens have not dried out?

✔ **Handouts**

Are handouts easily accessible and in order, so they can be distributed with minimum disruption? Have you arranged for assistance in handing them out if needed?

✔ **Microphones**

If speaking to more than 50 people you will probably need a microphone. Before your presentation you may want to request a microphone that allows you to move around. Request a broadcast lavelier mike that will hook on your jacket or tie and allow you to keep your hands free.

✔ **Lighting**

Try to leave on as much light as possible. Dimming the lights can contribute to people dozing off, especially after lunch.

✔ **Seating Arrangement**

If you have control over seating in the room, exercise it. If possible, arrange the seating so that the exit and entrance to the room are at the rear. In this way, if people come and go, it will cause the least amount of distraction.

If you know approximately how many people are going to be present, try to make sure that there are approximately as many seats as people. That way you won't have your audience sitting in the back of the room. Keeping your audience closer will focus their attention where you want it.

CHECKLIST FOR PRACTICING YOUR PRESENTATION

Following is a checklist for your practice sessions. Staying aware of these steps will help you give a more relaxed, confident, and enthusiastic presentation.

❑ Use your slides and overheads as "note cards" whenever possible. Remember, talk to the audience don't read to them.

❑ Mentally run through the presentation to review each idea in sequence, until you become familiar with the flow of ideas and where you plan to use slides to support them.

❑ Begin stand-up rehearsals of your presentation. Try to arrange a practice room similar to the one in which you will actually give your presentation.

❑ Give a simulated presentation, idea-for-idea (not word-for-word), using all slides.

❑ Strive for minimum focus on the notes, maximum focus on the audience.

❑ Practice answering the questions you anticipate from the audience.

❑ Give the full presentation again. If possible, videotape yourself or have a friend give you some feedback.

❑ Review the videotape and/or the friend's feedback and incorporate any necessary changes.

❑ Give one or two dress rehearsals of the presentation in its final form.

When You Can't Practice—
Successful Impromptu Speaking

Alex is invited, along with his manager, to attend a meeting of all department heads in the company. He is not expecting to say anything, only to sit and listen. During his manager's presentation, he is asked a question about the department's plans for the coming year. He turns to Alex and says, "Alex, you've been working on our major project for the past year. Maybe you could say a few words about how this project got started, where it stands, and where it is going."

If something like this happens to you, do not panic! You already know the fundamentals of organizing your thoughts, and you know your job. With these two resources you can effectively respond by taking the following steps:

Think:

Quickly formulate a simple position-action-benefit statement, then:

Plug into a pattern of organization. Any topic can be split up into components. Before you speak, break your topic into a pattern such as:

       A) past, present, and future (or any time-oriented combination),

       B) topic 1, 2, and 3 (e.g., production, advertising and marketing);

       C) the pro's and con's of an issue (useful in persuasive situations).

In Alex's case, the topic-ordered sequence is the best approach.

Then speak:

Start with the position, action, and benefit.

You will want to verbalize to yourself and your audience what your key points are. From the example above, Alex could simply state, "I would like to tell you about our production, advertising, and marketing departments."

➤ Deliver the body of the presentation.

➤ Talk through each point from your preview sentence. Having an organizational pattern established and knowing where you are going will take some of the stress out of the situation.

➤ If what you are speaking about is controversial, first acknowledge the opposition's case but finish with your viewpoint so you end by summarizing your position.

➤ Review the main points.

➤ Reinforce the main ideas you have touched upon by briefly restating them. Something like, 'I've tried in these past few minutes to give you an overview of our key departments, production, advertising, and marketing.'

➤ Conclude the presentation. Do not leave your audience high and dry. Conclude with a strong restatement of your position, action, and benefit.

SECTION REVIEW
PREPARING FOR YOUR PRESENTATION

1. Rehearse your presentation, standing up and using your slides.

2. Control the environment by checking:

   ❑ computer hardware and software

   ❑ seating arrangements

   ❑ lighting

   ❑ microphones

   ❑ handouts

   ❑ projection equipment to ensure it is available, in working condition, and has the required back-up supplies

3. When you have to give an impromptu presentation:

   ❑ develop a simple position, action, and benefit statement

   ❑ plug into a pattern of organization

   ❑ give a few introductory remarks

   ❑ preview and review the main points for your audience

   ❑ end with a strong restatement of position, action, and benefit

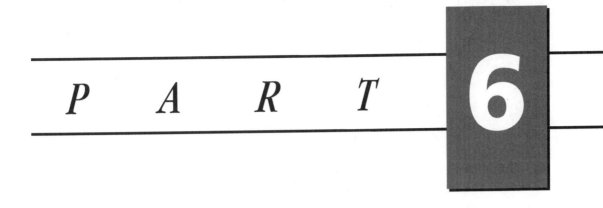

PART 6

Delivering Your Presentation with Energy and Composure

Engaging Your Audience

You must communicate your enthusiasm to the audience if you want them to be enthusiastic about the ideas you present, and that takes energy. Simultaneously, you must appear composed and confident in your demeanor.

It's not just what you say, but how you say it!

Standing stiffly, with little animation in your body, and speaking in a monotone voice without good eye contact is a sure way to deliver a speech that is a dud. We communicate with much more than words. Our nonverbal actions carry our feelings. If these channels get cut off because of anxiety, your interaction and rapport with the audience will suffer.

A great benefit of providing a natural and animated presentation style is that your nervous energy will flow in a positive form and not stay in your body. Seek a natural, conversational style; relate to people in the audience in a direct and personable manner, like you would in a dialogue situation. Even in the most formal presentation situations this is a necessity. The audience, and you, are most familiar with dialogue behavior—not monologue behavior. So, don't give the presentation in a stiff and unnatural manner.

You must learn to be aware of not only what you are saying but also how you are saying it. Learn to be your own coach while you are up in front of the audience, checking the items outlined in this section.

Putting Energy to Work

The following tips will help your presentation become animated, interesting, and engaging. If you can videotape a rehearsal, watch your delivery looking for the following items:

Movement

Typically, speakers tend to stand in one spot, feet rooted like a tree to the ground. If your presentation will be delivered from a lectern, try to get away from it! If appropriate, move to the side or front of the lectern to get nearer the audience. It is engaging, and audiences feel closer to the speaker without barriers in place. If you are using a microphone, then you will need an extension cord or lavelier mike. In a formal presentation, or if the lectern is at a head table, this technique may not be practical.

You should normally stay within four to six feet of the front row. Don't stay frozen in one spot but don't pace either. When you move always look at a person in the direction you are going. An occasional step to either side, or even a half-step towards the audience for emphasis, can enhance your presentation. Stay close, stay direct, and stay involved with your audience.

When delivering a presentation, keep your body facing the audience as much as possible. This will help keep your eye contact on the audience, where it should be. Body orientation becomes critical when using slides. You will have to angle away from the audience but it should not be more than 45 degrees. Don't speak unless you have eye contact with an audience member.

Gestures

The importance of natural gestures, uninhibited by anxiety, cannot by overstated. Too often anxiety holds back this important channel of communication. We use gestures for emphasis in normal conversation without thinking about what we are doing with our hands. Learn to gesture in front of an audience exactly as you would if you were having an animated conversation with a friend–nothing more, nothing less. Between gestures simply relax your hands to your sides–do not hold them up in front of you with your arms bent at the elbow.

Using natural gestures will not distract from a presentation; however, doing one of the following certainly will.

> ### DO NOT:
>
> • *Keep hands in your pockets*
>
> • *Keep hands "handcuffed" behind your back*
>
> • *Keep your arms crossed*
>
> • *Put hands in a "fig leaf" position*
>
> • *Wring your hands nervously*

Facial Expressions

Use them!

Voice

You need to stay aware of your volume. A soft voice may be perceived as showing a lack of confidence and hurt your credibility.

All vocal production starts with breathing. Breathe frequently and deeply to fuel your voice. When you speak, variety is the key. Vary your pitch, volume, and pacing, as you do in natural conversation or in storytelling. Your listeners will listen!

To find out if you have a volume problem before a presentation, ask someone who will give you a straight answer. Ask that person if you can be heard in the back of a room, if you trail off at the end of a sentence, or if you are speaking too loudly.

Too soft?

If your problem is a soft voice, there is a simple exercise to learn how to increase your volume. Recruit two friends to help you. Go into a room that is at least twice the size of the one where you normally give presentations. Have one person sit in the front row, and the other stand against the back wall. Start speaking, and have the person in the back give you a signal when you can be heard clearly. Note your volume level. How does it feel? Check with the person in the front row to make sure you were not too loud.

Most monotone voices are caused by anxiety. As the speaker tightens up, the muscles in the chest and throat become less flexible and air flow is restricted. When this happens, the voice loses its natural animation and a monotone results. To bring back the natural animation, you must relax and release tension. Upper and lower body movement are vital. This does not have to be dramatic movement—just enough to loosen the muscles and get you to breathe normally. Videotaping, audio taping, or feedback from a friend will let you know how you are doing.

Too loud?

A voice consistently too loud sometimes indicates a slight hearing loss. If your voice is judged too loud, you may wish to check with your doctor. If your hearing is okay, then do the above exercise again, but this time let the person in the front row give you a signal to soften your voice, and then check with the person in the back to make sure you can be heard.

When you have a large audience it is appropriate to ask during a presentation, "Can you hear me in the back?" The audience will usually be honest because they want to hear what you are saying!

Maintaining Composure

Posture

Keep your posture erect but relaxed. You want to stand up straight but not stiff. Your weight should be evenly distributed. Don't place your weight on one hip, then shift to the other and back again. This shifting can distract the audience.

Eye Contact

Speak to one person at a time when you present. Can you imagine interviewing a person who looked at the wall or floor when answering your questions? This would not inspire your confidence in that person. In our culture we expect good, direct eye contact. (Note: This is one of the biggest cultural variables, always find out what the audience is comfortable with if you are presenting in a culture outside your own.) Yet in many presentations, a speaker will look at a spot on the back of the wall, or at a screen, or at notes—everywhere but into the eyes of the audience.

Eye contact opens the channel of communication between people. It helps establish and build rapport. It involves the audience in the presentation, and makes the presentation more personable. Good eye contact between the speaker and audience also helps relax the speaker by connecting the speaker to the audience and reducing the speaker's feeling of isolation.

3 to 5 seconds per person

The rule of thumb for eye contact is three to five seconds per person. Try not to let your eyes dart around the room. Try to focus on one person, not long enough to make that individual feel uncomfortable, but long enough to pull him or her into your presentation. Then move on to another person.

When you give a presentation, don't just look at your audience—see them. Seek out individuals, and be aware that you are looking at them.

If the group is too large to look at each individual separately, make eye contact with individuals in different parts of the audience. People sitting near the individuals you select will feel that you are actually looking at them. As the distance between a speaker and audience increases, a larger and larger circle of people will feel your "eye contact."

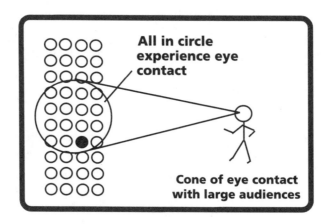

Pace

Our average conversational rate of speech is about 125 words per minute. When we become anxious, that rate will usually increase. An increased rate of speech is not necessarily a problem if your articulation is good. However, if you are delivering a technical presentation, or one in which the audience needs to take notes, you need to watch your pace.

Another indication that you are talking too fast is when you trip over words. When this happens, slow down. Listen for yourself to say the last word of a sentence, pause where the period would be, and then proceed to your next sentence.

Pausing

Pausing during a presentation can be an effective device to allow your important points to sink in. Don't be afraid to allow periods of silence during your presentation. The audience needs time to digest what you are saying. Use this time to take a breath and relax a moment.

Use a pause to fill those spaces that you might otherwise fill with sounds like: umm, ahh, and ah. A moment of silence will be a lot less distracting for your audience than those annoying "verbal tics."

Learn to listen to yourself; stay aware not only of *what* you are saying but also *how* you are saying it.

Question-and-Answer Techniques

Encouraging Your Audience to Ask Questions

Most presentations include time for audience questions during the session or at the end. In many cases the speaker has the option of when to have questions asked. If this is the case, ask the audience to interrupt you whenever they have questions, or request they save questions until you have finished the presentation. When you have delivered technical information, complicated ideas, or are leading a training session, it is a good idea to check audience comprehension by taking questions.

If you ask for questions passively, you will not encourage a response. This is often just a matter of body language. Standing away from the audience, hands stuffed in your pockets, and mumbling "Any questions?" does not encourage questions from an audience.

Those who actively seek questions will step toward the audience, raise a hand and ask, "Does anyone have questions for me?" You might also ask, "What questions do you have?" You assume the audience will ask questions, and they often do. Also pause long enough after asking for questions, so the audience will have time to think of questions (the silence should get to them before it gets to you!) Raising your hand will accomplish two things. One, it is the visual signal for questions and will encourage those who might be shy. Also, it helps keep order. The audience will follow your lead and raise their hands, instead of yelling out their questions.

Listening Attentively to Questions

Perhaps you have seen a speaker listen to a question while pacing back and forth, not looking at the person asking the question. The speaker may not know what is being asked until the question is finished. It is important to wait until the questioner has finished.

While the question is being asked, you should watch the person who is asking it. Often it is possible to pick up clues to the intensity of the question, the feelings behind it, and any hidden agendas. Pay attention to the questioner's body language.

During questions, be careful what you do with your hands! Imagine giving a presentation enthusiastically, and presenting your ideas confidently. Then imagine that when you receive a question, you stand looking at the floor rubbing your hands together nervously. This behavior can negate the confident image you provided during the presentation. Your hands should stay in a neutral position, arms at your sides, fingers open. Focus on the question and listen carefully.

Answering Questions

Prepare for questions.

You should be able to anticipate most of the questions you receive. Practice answering them. Prepare for the worst and everything else will seem easier. Some speakers prepare back-up visual aids, to be used specifically when answering anticipated questions.

Don't preface your answer.

When a speaker starts an answer with, "That's a very good question; I'm glad you asked it," it may be a sign that the speaker is unsure of the answer. At the end of your question-and-answer session you can say something like, "Thank you for all your excellent questions."

Clarify.

If the question you receive is lengthy or complex, restate it for clarification. This may not be necessary, if the question is simple and straightforward. But sometimes, people are thinking aloud as they formulate their questions and even the most simple inquiry may become confusing as it is buried in 17 paragraphs of their commentary. Clarifying can also allow you to soften hostile language used in the question and give you more time to consider your answer.

Amplify.

Have you ever been sitting in the back of an audience and someone in the front row asks a question and you can't hear it? If in doubt you might want to repeat the question so that you are sure everyone heard it. This technique can also give you extra thinking time.

Maintain your style.

When answering questions, it is important to maintain the same style and demeanor you used in the presentation. A change in demeanor can suggest that you are not confident about your position.

Be honest.

If you don't know the answer to a question, simply say, "I don't know the answer but I will find out and get back to you." Or, if co-workers might know the answer, you can ask them for help.

Involve the whole audience in your answer.

Have you seen speakers who get involved with the person who has asked a question and ignore the rest of the audience? In some situations the questioner may try to "hook" the speaker with a difficult question. You can always tell if a speaker is "hooked" because he or she focuses only on the person who asked the question.

Employ the 25%–75% rule.

Direct approximately 25% of your eye contact to the person who asked the question and approximately 75% to the rest of the audience. (This is especially important in a hostile question-and-answer situation.) Don't ignore the person who asked the question *or* the rest of the audience. This will help you stay in command of the situation and keep the audience involved in your presentation.

Keep answers to the point.

Don't belabor an issue. Make your answer long enough to cover the subject but short enough to be interesting!

Dealing With Hostile Questions

Let's face it, sometimes people in the audience are upset or angry and they are going to take it out on you. It is probably one of the more difficult situations speakers face. Here is a three-step process for dealing with tough situations:

Acknowledge feelings, fact, or both

For example, someone asks, "Why did you screw up and go 40% over budget?"

Using this technique, you would begin your answer by saying something like, "Mike, it's true, we did go over budget and I know you are upset about it." Notice that this reply is non-defensive and avoids escalating the situation.

Respond with information

At this point explain what happened with the facts of the situation. "As some of you may know, we had the opportunity to make a very large bid. In order to prepare the bid we had to purchase five new computer systems. I am happy to report that it was an excellent investment, albeit over budget, because we won the bid."

Maintain position

At this point it is imperative that you restate your original position sentence. (You already have the wording—remember, Position-Action-Benefit). Finish with a strong statement of your stance on the issue. Something like, "Therefore, I maintain that we should have a 50% budget increase next year."

REVIEW CHECKLIST
DELIVERING YOUR PRESENTATION

I plan to:

- ❏ Stay aware of not only what is said, but also how I say it

- ❏ Be animated, enthusiastic, and direct in my delivery

- ❏ Use eye contact to make my presentation personable and conversational

- ❏ Keep a clear, strong voice and not speak too fast

QUESTION-AND-ANSWER TECHNIQUES

I plan to:

- ❏ Ask for questions by stepping forward with my hand raised

- ❏ Anticipate questions and practice the answers

- ❏ Watch the questioner and listen carefully to the question

- ❏ Keep my hands in a neutral position when listening to questions

- ❏ Repeat the question to make sure everyone heard it or for clarification

- ❏ Keep the same style and demeanor that I had during the presentation

- ❏ Use eye contact and involve the whole audience in my answer

Final Review Checklist

Check (✓) the following items as you prepare and then deliver your presentation.

✔ **To deal with anxiety, I plan to:**

- ❑ Breathe deeply
- ❑ Focus on relaxing
- ❑ Release tension by unobtrusive isometrics
- ❑ Move during the presentation
- ❑ Maintain good eye contact with the audience

✔ **To plan and organize my presentation, I will:**

- ❑ Analyze my audience
- ❑ Develop Position, Action, Benefit statements
- ❑ Brainstorm main ideas
- ❑ Brainstorm subpoints
- ❑ Structure my introduction
- ❑ Develop a strong conclusion
- ❑ Formulate the main idea, preview/review sentence
- ❑ Develop slides and other visual aids
- ❑ Develop handouts

✔ **To develop and use visual aids, I expect to:**

- ❑ Use the K.IS.S. principal
- ❑ Choose the correct type of chart
- ❑ Use appropriate titles
- ❑ Refrain from talking to the visual aids
- ❑ Place myself at center stage
- ❑ Use my pointer sparingly

✔ **To prepare for the presentation, I will:**

- ❑ Rehearse standing up and using visuals
- ❑ Check seating, the AV equipment, all handouts, etc.

✔ **While delivering my presentation, I plan to:**

- ❑ Stay aware of what I am saying and how I say it
- ❑ Be animated, enthusiastic, and direct
- ❑ Make my presentation personable and conversational
- ❑ Use a clear, strong voice

✔ **For question-and-answer sessions, I plan to:**

- ❑ Raise my hand and step towards the audience
- ❑ Watch and listen to the questioner
- ❑ Repeat the question if necessary
- ❑ Maintain my style and demeanor
- ❑ Answer to the whole audience with my eye contact

NOTES

NOTES

NOTES

NOTES

NOTES

94

NOTES

VERL

CRISP WORLDWIDE DISTRIBUTION

English language books are distributed worldwide. Major international distributors include:

ASIA/PACIFIC

Australia/New Zealand: In Learning, PO Box 1051, Springwood QLD, Brisbane, Australia 4127   Tel: 61-7-3-841-2286, Facsimile: 61-7-3-841-1580
ATTN: Messrs. Richard/Robert Gordon

Hong Kong/Mainland China: Crisp Learning Solutions, 18/F Honest Motors Building 9-11 Leighton Rd., Causeway Bay, Hong Kong   Tel: 852-2915-7119, Facsimile: 852-2865-2815 ATTN: Ms. Grace Lee

Indonesia: Pt Lutan Edukasi, Citra Graha, 7th Floor, Suite 701A, Jl. Jend. Gato Subroto Kav. 35-36, Jakarta 12950 Indonesia Tel: 62-21-527-9060/527-9061 Facsimile: 62-21-527-9062 ATTN: Mr. Suwardi Luis

Japan: Phoenix Associates, Believe Mita Bldg., 8th Floor 3-43-16 Shiba, Minato-ku, Tokyo 105-0014, Japan   Tel: 81-3-5427-6231, Facsimile: 81-3-5427-6232
ATTN: Mr. Peter Owans

Malaysia, Philippines, Singapore: Epsys Pte Ltd., 540 Sims Ave #04-01, Sims Avenue Centre, 387603, Singapore   Tel: 65-747-1964, Facsimile: 65-747-0162 ATTN: Mr. Jack Chin

CANADA

Crisp Learning Canada, 60 Briarwood Avenue, Mississauga, ON L5G 3N6 Canada Tel: 905-274-5678, Facsimile: 905-278-2801 ATTN: Mr. Steve Connolly

EUROPEAN UNION

England: Flex Learning Media, Ltd., 9-15 Hitchin Street, Baldock, Hertfordshire, SG7 6AL, England
Tel: 44-1-46-289-6000, Facsimile: 44-1-46-289-2417   ATTN: Mr. David Willetts

INDIA

Multi-Media HRD, Pvt. Ltd., National House, Floor 1, 6 Tulloch Road, Appolo Bunder, Bombay, India 400-039 Tel: 91-22-204-2281, Facsimile: 91-22-283-6478 ATTN: Messrs. Ajay Aggarwal/ C.L. Aggarwal

SOUTH AMERICA

Mexico: Grupo Editorial Iberoamerica, Nebraska 199, Col. Napoles, 03810 Mexico, D.F. Tel: 525-523-0994, Facsimile: 525-543-1173   ATTN: Señor Nicholas Grepe

SOUTH AFRICA

Corporate: Learning Resources, PO Box 2806, Parklands, Johannesburg 2121, South Africa, Tel: 27-21-531-2923, Facsimile: 27-21-531-2944 ATTN: Mr. Ricky Robinson

MIDDLE EAST

Edutech Middle East, L.L.C., PO Box 52334, Dubai U.A.E.
Tel: 971-4-359-1222, Facsimile: 971-4-359-6500   ATTN: Mr. A.S.F. Karim